Dump him,
Marry the CAT!

Dump him,
Marry the CAT!

Why A Cat is a Better Match Than A Man

WILLOW CREEK PRESS

Published by Willow Creek Press
P.O. Box 147, Minocqua, Wisconsin 54548

Page 2 photo © Klein & Hubert/BIOS/Peter Arnold, Inc.
Editor: Andrea Donner
Design: Donnie Rubo

Printed in Canada

To Scooter

SURE, men are great...

Once in a while, when somebody's MOTHER did a good job, you'll find a MAN who is kind, intelligent, funny, attractive, polite, AND loyal. HOWEVER, at other times, a woman is better off just hanging out with her CAT, who is all of these things and MORE. There are countless reasons WHY A CAT IS A BETTER MATCH THAN A MAN. Here are just a few...

For starters,

a cat is
dependable...

doesn't channel surf...

loves your attention...

...and is always happy
to receive a special treat.

A cat is also always happy to see you...

...and never feels crowded.

He looks at you when you are talking to him...

makes you laugh...

LISTENS...

and doesn't pick fights.

He is loyal...

authentic...

honest...

mysterious...

AND, has plenty of hair.

He hisses at others (not at you)...

has cute feet (not stinky ones)...

and loves to cuddle.

A cat is easy to amuse...

and yet can entertain himself.

He doesn't hide his feelings...

but will always let you know how he feels.

A cat is affectionate (even in public)...

devoted...

and he doesn't care one iota how you look...

or how much you weigh.

He melts your heart with his sweetness...

he readily forgives...

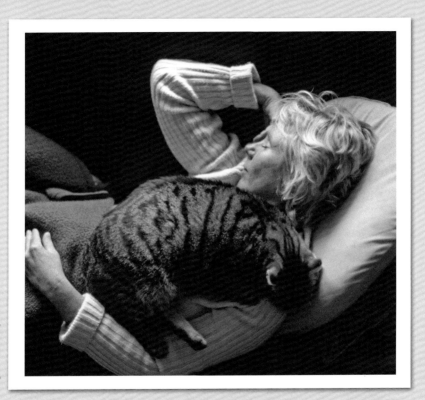

he's warm...

and even if he does lay
around the house all day...

at least he doesn't make a mess.

SURE, cats can be a lot of work...

They need to be fed, bathed, brushed, coddled, babied, taken to the doctor when they're sick, encouraged, supported, cleaned up after, and made to feel they are the absolute MOST important being in your life...

But, HOW is that different than a man?

At least a cat will help with the dishes...

has no clothes to wash...

will help
dust the
high places...

and keep unwanted pests out of the house.

He loves
a good
scratch...

but he can do it himself too.

A cat is easy to please...

tender-hearted...

fun-loving...

and confident.

He's ALWAYS interested in what you're reading.

A cat doesn't mind girl talk...

and can keep a secret.

He's great
with kids...

and tolerates dogs.

He gives you your space...

but is there when you need him.

A cat sees nothing wrong
with spoiling yourself...

and agrees that each of
you is a superior being.

He doesn't want you to leave...

and yet he's
perfectly
capable of
taking care
of himself.

He never steals the blankets...

has "cute" bad breath...

is patient when you're busy...

and won't make fun of
your stuffed animal collection.

He's happy to join you on a midnight snack attack...

and will sleep late with you on the weekends.

He keeps
himself
impeccably
clean...

he's interested in your hobbies...

and when he goes out for the night...

you know he'll be home by morning.

A cat is also a good judge of character...

© Cris Kelly

and doesn't care if you're in love
with more than one of them.

He waits for you to come home...

and greets you when you return.

A cat
doesn't care
if you go
shopping
all day...

and watch sentimental movies all night.

He's content with just a squeak ball...

a nap...

or just your attention.

He loves to play...

but will be your perfect companion if you
want to spend all day doing nothing.

He'll console you when you're down...

and he'll never leave you for a younger cat!

OK, so a MAN will never be as good as a CAT...

But that doesn't mean you shouldn't love him or marry him. Just make sure your MAN gives you...

all of the RESPECT...

friendship...

and unconditional LOVE that a cat would
(and that you deserve)!